EGYPT

SMITHMARK

Text
Simonetta Crescimbene

Graphic design
Patrizia Balocco

Contents

2-3 *The three imposing pyramids of Giza are dedicated to three pharaohs respectively: Cheops, Chephren, and Mycerinus. Built during the fourth dynasty, they are lined up by size from northeast to southwest.*

4-5 *In Abu Simbel are two rock temples, saved from the waters of Lake Nasser. The "eviction" of the temples of Rameses II and Nefertiti took over 1,000 workers more than six years. The removal was completed in 1968.*

6 *Daraw, near Aswan, gets busy with feverish sales on the occasion of the camel market.*

7 *The image of this bas-relief comes from Karnak, privileged pole of the sun cult. On the occasion of the feast of the New Year, the magnificent procession of the god Amon started here.*

8-9 *The white-sailed felucca is one of the most important features of Egypt's rivers.*

10-11 *This photograph shows a moment of trade in At Daraw, the camel market "at the gates of Africa." The same colours that influenced the "orientalist" painters of the past century and are indelible in our memory are still bright and unchanged in reality.*

12-13 *The most ancient monasteries in the world are in the Egyptian desert. The first Christian monks and hermits found shelter and protection here. In those times defensive measures were necessary, so buildings assumed fortresslike features, as shown in this picture of the Coptic monastery of Wadi Natrun.*

14-15 *A great number of Egyptian people live in Cairo, the capital city, which is the model of religion, social status, and local colour of the whole country.*

This edition published in 1996 by SMITHMARK Publishers, a division of U.S. Media Holdings Inc., 16 East 32nd Street, New York, NY 10016.

SMITHMARK books are available for bulk purchase for sales promotion and premium use. For details write or call the manager of special sales, SMITHMARK Publishers, 16 East 32nd Street, New York, NY 10016; (212) 532-6600.

First published by Edizioni White Star.
Title of the original edition: Egitto, lungo il fiume della civiltà.
© World copyright 1993 by Edizioni White Star.
Via Candido Sassone 24, 13100 Vercelli, Italy.

ISBN 0-8317-3565-1

Printed in Singapore by Tien Wah Press.

Introduction

"And so this is Egypt, land of the pharaohs, land of the Ptolemys, home of Cleopatra." With these words, Maxime Du Camp began his book, "Egypte, Nubie, Palestine et Syrie." Published in 1852, it was one of the first photographic travel books to present, to the avidly Romantic gaze of the mid-nineteenth-century French reader, images of white feluccas with gracefully bellying sails, huge sand-coloured ruins, palm groves, and endless dust. The land of Egypt has been accorded the same refined accolades in travel journals, broadsheets, prose, and poetry of every age - in the works of Count Constantin François Volney (a French republican intellectual and savant who was a senator under Napoleon), Edward William Lane (an Arabic scholar and translator of the Koran and the Thousand and One Nights, who lived for a while in Cairo under the name of Mansur Effendi), Alphonse de Lamartine (French poet and statesman), Théophile Gautier, and William Shakespeare - all those who, like Gustave Flaubert, yearned after the East, "dancing at the edge of their desk"

When Du Camp published his book, France was still recovering from the scars and self-doubt of the revolution, just five decades earlier. The French looked outward - "elsewhere" - in hopes of shaking off the cold and brutal tradition of the Jacobins and the Terror. What better alternative than a mysterious and aromatic land full of sphinxes, chimeras, and mysterious rituals? Travel to this exotic and esoteric world was equivalent to initiation into a different system of values, at least to the eager Romantics of a century or so past. Still, Egypt was hardly an unknown land to Europeans of the last century. As early as 1810, Chateaubriand wrote, "And what can I say about Egypt? Who has not already seen it?"

Over the centuries, a small upper-class army of "cultural tourists" has trodden Egyptian soil, in the time-honoured tradition of an apprenticeship in the land of wisdom. Many a scholar and thinker walked in the (legendary) footsteps of Thales, Solon, Aesop, Lycurgus, Alcaeus, Democritus, Pythagoras, and Plato, all of whom had visited Egypt to learn more about the world. Plato, in his dialogue, "Timaeus," put words into the mouth of the senior Egyptian priest, who exclaimed, "Solon! Solon! You Greeks are eternal children and you have a childish soul." The priestly caste is described with admiration by Diodorus Siculus as being devoted to the search of knowledge. He calls the library of the temples a "clinic for the soul." Some consternation appears, however, in the opinions that Greeks and Romans had formed of the deities these wise men worshipped. In a mix of amazement and scorn, Juvenal wrote, "Entire villages adore cats, or a freshwater fish, or else dogs. No one reveres Diana. It is sacrilege to dare to violate a leek or an onion, by biting them with one's teeth: oh blessed

peoples, who grow Gods in your gardens!" While the Latin poet, who was supposedly relegated to the command of a garrison in Upper Egypt, felt it was unseemly that the goddess Hathor should live in a sycamore tree, that the god Nefertem should resemble a lotus flower, or that the goddess of Bubastis was a cat and that of Buto a snake (the uraeus, or cobra), the time was simply not yet ripe. In later centuries, the European imagination fell under the thrall of the mystical allure of a desert civilization. In the fifteenth century, the Italian architect and scholar Leon Battista Alberti decyphered hieroglyphics, aided by an unhealthy and highly inaccurate dose of imagination. Francesco Colonna, with intricate conjectures and deductions, proclaimed himself a noble descendant of the Egyptian Hercules, in turn son to Isis and Osiris; the heraldic symbol of the Borgia family, a bull, suddenly turned into the bovine god Hapi, called Apis by the Greeks. In Rome during the baroque period, twelve obelisks became part of the city's fabric, a dozen improbable stone rays in a metaphorical papal sunburst, eloquent of Rome's ancient alliances and depredations.

A meandering, limitless past of mystical ties leads up to the modern age of technology - pilgrims to the land of magic now fly there, enjoying comfortable service and paying by credit card. The enchantment of Egypt for us is now filtered through a collective memory of film, as well - we expect to see armies of extras, like in the films of Lubitsch, Cecil B. De Mille, Mattoli, and Fracassi, and we want to see them live, no longer in flickering images.

Most of the fifty-seven million inhabitants of Egypt live and work along the green banks of the river Nile. Life is everywhere, sprawling over the green ribbon of the Nile, and leaving the majority of the country's 386,659 square miles to caravans of wandering nomads, vultures, and scorpions. Eighty per cent of the Egyptian population lives in the fertile delta, crowding right up to the Mediterranean Sea; each year many thousands of fellahin, or peasants, abandon their land and make their way to the great metropolis of Cairo. These peasants who desert the *shaduf* (a hand-operated pivoted lever with a weight at one end counterbalancing the bucket at the other) and the *tambur* (a primitive, lever-operated device that has been used as a pump in irrigation since the time of the New Kingdom, three millennia past; basically, an Archimedean screw) confound the unfortunate Egyptian census-takers, already discouraged by the ballooning birthrate: a new Egyptian is born every twenty-five seconds. The best estimates probably conservative - state that Cairo has thirteen million inhabitants, who must compete with another four million commuters for transportation and jobs. In 1898, a traveller named Eduard Schuré wrote this about Cairo: "A foreigner who throws himself into this rushing stream is immediately swept away in a whirlpool of people of all

16 *A meditative Bedouin tugs on the dense, aromatic smoke of the narghile. This picture of Levantine leisure can be glimpsed everywhere: in the intricate alleys of the bazaar, where shopkeepers wait patiently for customers, and at rest stops along the dusty caravan routes.*

17 top *Egyptian marketplaces are a blend of lively "swap meets" and more traditional commerce; here the nation purchases its basic needs, and stops to gossip and chat. This photograph shows the marketplace of Luxor.*

17 bottom *In Cairo, intense motor traffic often grinds to a halt; traffic jams and endless queues are the prevailing rule. Speed is not of the essence, and so many choose a more traditional means of conveyance, both reliable and inexpensive.*

18-19 *Modern civilization may have developed fast, fuel-driven vehicles, but nomads and fellahs rely on the venerable camels and dromedaries.*

20 top *In Dandarah, one can visit a temple, built during the dynasty of the Ptolemys, dedicated to the goddess Hathor. The present building dates to the Ptolemaic period and was completed by Augustus, but rests on the site of a far earlier foundation.*

20 bottom *The temple of Nefertari, Rameses's royal bride, at Abu Simbel stands just a few hundred feet from the magnificent temple dedicated to her husband.*

21 top *In the temple of Rameses II, at Abu Simbel, the pharaoh's features were carved into the impressive pillars that support the richly ornamented vaults.*

21 bottom *This boulevard, lined with human-headed sphinxes, leads to the temple of Amon, at Luxor.*

22-23 *On the east bank of the Nile, not far from Luxor, stands the vast temple complex of Karnak, one of the largest archaeological sites in the world.*

24-25 *This overhead view the complex arrangement of the necropolis of Thebes.*

races. In the space of a few minutes, he will see tall, fine-featured Abyssinians draped in white garb; coffee-coloured Nubians with sensual lips; laughing lively fellahs with their loose blue smocks; Armenians in black turbans, serious as monks; handsome, nimble Syrians with large luminous eyes; aristocratic, haughty Persians; sullen Copts; Jews with humble, penetrating eyes; proud Arabs and Bedouins in rags."

The fact that Egypt is such a polyglot, polyethnic nation is certainly due in part to the long-ago dawning of civilization, when men were judged by their cultural depth and their civic responsibility. Egypt of the pharaohs was profoundly influenced by Mesopotamia - it was in regular contact with Crete, it was toured by Greeks on their equivalent of the Grand Tour, it traded with the Nubians for ebony, ivory, leopard skins, and giraffe tails, and commerce with Syria brought in swords, helmets, and chariots. Trade as they might, however, the Egyptians never developed a military culture sufficient to allow them to stave off the invasions of their warlike neighbours. Modern Egypt almost seems to cleave to the same wisdom, and Islam - which considers individualism to be arrogant and sinful - reiterates the lesson. In the poorer quarters of Cairo, all seem to obey the impulse to offer hospitality. Apartment dwellers share their living space, and still offer to sublet, while city roofs sprout tents and straw screens, to ensure "penthouse" privacy. Under the weight of this onslaught of new arrivals, more than one building has collapsed. The city government resignedly publishes statistics showing the worrisome state of affairs - 80 per cent of the houses built in the last decade are "informal," illegally built, and structurally unreliable. Those who cannot find living quarters in the city of the living have turned to the "towns of the dead" - El Imanel-Shafi, Bab el-Wazir Mohamad, El Migawirin, and Bab al Nasr Mohamad are the names of four Muslim cemeteries on the east side of Cairo, where newly arrived peasants, scrimping students, and evicted tenants have found new homes in funerary vaults. Vast armies of graveyard tenants now occupy these cemeteries, creating small cities on their own - there are workshops, vegetable stalls, chicken coops, and little gardens everywhere. And now there are little shantytowns springing up outside the cemeteries, where those who cannot find a place inside are making do, sheltering in the shade of the walls. The population explosion shows no signs of flagging, and the forecasts are cataclysmic. Growing poverty awaits, and yet an old Egyptian proverb says, "Children are the wealth of Egypt." Twenty-five per cent of the population of Cairo is under the age of six, and it is unthinkable to try to force the poor to give up one of their prime resources, the manpower - or childpower - that is so vital in making ends meet. It will not be a simple task to reform the economy of a nation that is burdened with inadequate infrastructure and whose public service sector has to

make do with too little for too many. The hordes of civil servants and ministry employees that constitute more of a giant traffic jam than a work force are for the most part college graduates. The idea of employing them was Gamal Abdel Nasser's. His intention was to reduce the number of unemployed intellectuals; some 90 per cent of the jobless in the newest generation have at least finished high school. A symptom of widespread discontent is certainly fundamentalist extremism; extremists blame a westward-leaning political line for the weakness of the economy, saying that capitalism is undermining the Islamic identity. The fundamentalist fringe encourages acts of violence among those who wish to see Islamic principles put into operation in the political, economic, and social life of the nation. And in 1981, a crushing blow was administered to the stability of the Egyptian state. During a military review in the heart of Heliopolis, President Anwar Sadat was assassinated in full view of the public and of television cameras. Those images of mayhem, etched into our collective memory, contrast sharply with the Islamic ideals of moderation and harmony. Those ideals, however, are not lost entirely. They can still be glimpsed in the patient smiles of the homeless and poor, in the seraphic confidence of those who consider haste to be the Devil's errand ("patience is Allah's," they intone), or in the resourcefulness of those who invent bizarre trades at every street corner. Egyptian society seems to be a castle of contradictions - at every level of daily life there is a dichotomy. Fundamentalists and western thinkers, Muslims and Copts, the penniless and the rich live side by side under the eternal, cerulean blue sky, from Alexandria to Aswan. Cairo, which is a microcosm of the entire nation, perhaps displays the ultimate paradox. Although its inhabitants are desperately needy, it is a safe city. In this land, poverty engenders dignity and pride, and the traveller can venture safely through the heart of the city at any hour. An evening visit to Khan el Khalili, the oldest and largest bazaar in the city, is obligatory for those who want to embrace the authentic spirit of the East. The bazaar is a surging sea of humanity, and the elbowing and shoving fits in perfectly with the frantic haggling and bartering. Even the sounds - glottal stops, clicking "q"s, and grating "r"s - seem to soar and tumble. Dramatic quarrels and angry accusations are not what they seem; it is just consummate playacting that is part of an ancient commercial ritual, an intricate exchange of courtesy and merchandise set amidst stalls groaning with fabrics and objects straight out of the "Thousand and One Nights." Glimmering, swaying lamps cast uncertain reflections on copper and brass. A line of lamps curves off into the distance and disappears around a corner. The line of dim light stops, and there a small knot of do-nothings, untouched by all the frenetic activity, suck meditatively on their hookah, emitting puffs of aromatic smoke into the glittering levantine night. Further along, tailors bend over their work with a half-smile, stitched silks and brocades; metal workers hammer away, speaking loudly and animatedly all the while and occasionally waving their tools in an effort to lure Arab or European customers. Added to the welter of sounds and sights are myriad aromas - pungent spices, the sweet and musky scents of oils and essences. In the "Street of Gold," silver and semiprecious stones are hammered, carved, and polished with inborn skill by the heirs to those craftsmen of dozens of centuries ago developed two hundred and seventy-five different shapes for amulets (at least, that is how many have been recorded), made of materials ranging from faïence to carnelian, obsidian, serpentine, or lapis lazuli. In visiting this marketplace named after Khalil - the sultan who first decreed its existence, in 1292 - one should pay as much attention to the small streets that can barely contain the antiques shops and souvenir stands as to the shops themselves. There is a folk museum which stands in a ancient warehouse, surely dating from the middle ages. And there are a great many ateliers of artists; here in Cairo, these artists have an illustrious patron and colleague in artistic experimentation, Farouk Hosni by name, and minister of culture by official title.

This city, over a thousand years old, knew its moment of greatest splendour and wealth in mediaeval times. Cairo was then considered the largest and most opulent city in the known world. One can still glimpse relics of that magnificent time, tucked away behind austere facades in the oldest neighbourhoods of the "Muslim" quarter. Seen from the outside, little can be glimpsed but massive and featureless walls, broken here and there by windows covered by arabesques of carved wood. Behind those dense wooden screens are the women's quarters; in the tradition of the veil, the women could look out without being seen. On the inside, where merchants and aristocrats once lived in pleasant shade and coolness, the rooms are arrayed around the "qaa," a small courtyard that offers a rectangle of brighter light in which to receive guests. Again, wooden screens allowed mothers, sisters, and courtesans to watch, unseen, while business meetings or parties went on in the central room. In the centre of this room stood a stone fountain, with its jets, sprays, and cascades of water. Egyptian architects were particularly proud to show off the most precious element, especially in a desert land - water. Furnishings that we would find more ordinary adorn the walls and floor. Multicoloured marble compositions, stained glass arabesques, graceful furniture made of wood and burnished metal can be admired in the houses of Shabshiri and Gamal el-din ed-Dahabi, in the palaces of the Emirs Radwan Bey and Beshtaq, and in many others, some of which are perfectly preserved, while others have been expertly

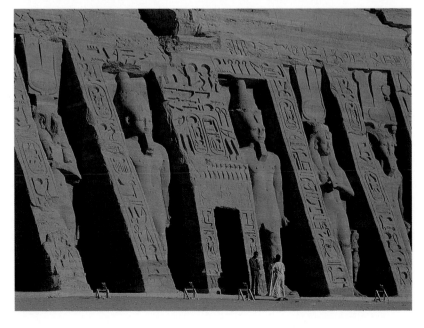

restored. All of these remarkable residences stand just to the north of the Gate of Bab al Zuweila. And if the visitor wishes to savour the "culture" of the neighbourhood, one excellent way is to sit for a spell at the small table of a cafe; a brief interlude at the Fichawi, with no tourist activites whatever, can be an excellent idea for European, American, and Japanese "speed travellers" overwhelmed by their package tours and by the unbroken exposure to Amon, the sun god. The men (only men) who frequent this cafe spend hours and hours amidst the smoke of the narghiles, which rises, slowly and ineluctably, toward the ceiling, reflected in the huge mirrors. And the excellent mint tea can help create an aura of exoticism that is, after all, the basis of a good vacation. You may choose to sit at the favourite table of Naguib Mahfouz, Nobel Laureate for literature in 1988, and you can conjure up images of the Cairene intellectuals who spent time here, talking and writing, in the thirties and fifties. As groups of tourists emerge from the Fichawi at nightfall, they are often startled by the stentorian voices of the muezzins, now often broadcast in stereo, from the tops of the towers that stud the "city of a thousand minarets." Actually, there are "only" six hundred; their vertical structure creates a splendid network of mosques over the skyline of Cairo. The great university mosque of Al Azhar sprawls massively over two and a half acres of ground; it boasts five minarets, three hundred pillars, and six monumental doors - it has offered haven for spiritual reflection and prayer since A.D. 970. Nearby, the "splendid one" - as it is called - is home to the oldest and most prestigious university in the Arab world, a centre for higher Islamic theological studies. It possesses a library that is certainly equal to the responsibilities that the Islamic world has attributed to it over the centuries. The library contains fifteen thousand manuscripts on topics including astronomy, philosophy, medicine, chemistry, and various other subjects. Today, twenty thousand students from all over Muslim Africa and Asia study here (there is a separate section for women) in nine different departments. The four schools of Koranic law, the Hanafi, the Maliki, the Shafi'i, and the Hanbali are studied and expounded in the madrasa, or religious school, that was founded by the Sultan Hasan. This building, which dates back to the time of the Mamelukes (1356-1362) has often been used as a citadel, given its imposing size and massive structure. It has been used as a school, a mosque, and a fortress, but the elegance of its form and the grace of its decorations in relief has not been diminished. Seventy oil lamps made of finely worked iridescent glass have been removed from the heavy chains upon which they hung from the vault, and are now on display in the Museum of Islamic Art. Opposite stands a modern construction - the mosque of Al Rifa'i, completed in 1912, where rest the remains of Kings Fuad and Farouk and of the Shah

of Iran, Reza Pahlevi. Not far off, facing a narrow alley, is yet another place of worship. Inside, the walls blossom with Italian marble and Persian majolica in shades of green and blue: a cool-toned garden of imagination that has earned the name of the Blue Mosque. Islamic art is unlikely to disappoint even the most demanding explorer, whether they are aesthetes in search of the finest carvings and screenwork or simply curious travellers who love learned anecdotes or historical oddities. In the mosque of Ibn Tulun, which dates from A.D. 876, there is a long frieze bearing Kufic letters, said to contain a complete edition of the Koran! Although this is one of the most ancient forms of Arabic writing, it seems unlikely that the wooden structure beneath it is made of wood from Noah's Ark, as some suggest. Equally improbable hypotheses concern the construction of the mosque of Amr, the oldest in the city - the mosque was built in A.D. 642, and among the pillars supporting the ceiling stands one said to have been carried miraculously there from Mecca by Mohammed himself. Two other pillars, popularly termed the "pillars of testing," are reputed to oppose the presence of sinners and to accept with tranquillity that of the virtuous. We are now in the heart of "Old Cairo," the neighbourhood of the Christian community which stands in the oldest structure in the city - inside the walls of the Roman fortress on the Nile. Little is discarded by Egyptian culture, which studies and preserves with painstaking care or dogmatic fervour the stratifications of religions and ideologies. The alternation of religious movements of great social importance has led to a survival - though as a minority - of many distinctive features and artistic idiosyncracies. The bizarre Egyptian dynasty of deities, dating from 3000 B.C., had its roots in a number of divine "nuclear families." One of the most important was Isis, Osiris, and Horus; in later times, the trio took on the seminal role of Holy Trinity. Less important but far more numerous, a crazy-quilt roster of minor and more human gods, worshipped by what we would call the working classes, extended their tutelary influence over a number of professions and activities. Thus, the ram-god Khnum moulded each and every child on his potter's wheel before birth, the seven goddesses Hathor told each child his destiny, the god Bes, a dancing dwarf who made children laugh, gave humanity celebration, joy, and protection from the evil-minded, the snake goddess Mertseger warded off harm from the labourers in the Theban necropolis.... In the courtyards of the sanctuaries, the faithful would place offerings and little votive steles, upon which were engraved ears - just one or a great many, depending on the urgency - to supplicate assistance from the appropriate divinities. Modern-day Egyptians, especially the fellahin, or peasants, sometimes seek to communicate with these ancient gods; in order to do so, they undertake pilgrimages to the appropriate tombs and temples.

In 1379 B.C., the pharaoh Amenhotep IV changed his name to Ikhnaton and started a religion that was, at first glance, merely religious, but which ultimately had sweeping political repercussions. Ikhnaton invented a monotheistic religion, and in so doing diminished the temporal power of the Theban priests. These priests had little choice, at first, but honour the new "neb taui" (lord of the two lands) and the sun god Aton.

The older, polytheistic religion and the regime of the priests, however, was later restored, and the people once again prayed to their many and bizarre idols. Then, must we conclude that the heretic pharaoh failed in his attempt to change the course of history? Great thinkers have claimed that Ikhnaton was, in a certain sense, the original founder of Christianity. Sigmund Freud has theorized that Ikhnaton was an influential reformer who changed the face of early civilization; the intriguing thesis has even been put forth that Moses - raised and educated at the court of Egypt, according to Holy Scriptures - had enjoyed the hospitality of the reformer pharaoh. Historians and Scripture-hounds visiting Egypt can study the landscapes where some of the most crucial episodes in the Bible took place, from the exodus of the Hebrews toward Canaan to the parting of the waters of the Red Sea. In the Sinai desert, the Greek Orthodox monastery of Saint Catherine still stands on the site where the emperor Justinian ordered it erected in A.D. 527, in the belief that there God revealed himself to Moses in the form of a burning bush, and handed down the Tablets of the Ten Commandments. From the monastery, three thousand steps carved into the rock by penitent monks - and just climbing them seems like sufficient mortification of the flesh - climb up to the peak of the Mount of Moses. There are other remarkable monasteries in the Sinai desert - Saint Anthony's is the oldest Coptic monastery, and was founded in the third century by the followers of the hermit saint. The White Monastery owes its remarkable makeup to the entrepreneurial spirit of a determined and inspired monk named Scenute. The three, rather exotic naves of the basilica are supported by unmatched pillars that bear hieroglyphics; they were in fact borrowed from the nearby archaic monument, Athribis. The floors of the monastery are likewise made of massive blocks of granite from another "heathen" Egyptian religious monument.

Let us return now to the worn and time-laden Roman walls of the "old part" of Cairo, and examine the historical ties to the ancient Jewish community of this part of the world. Legend has it that the small dank crypt beneath the transept of the church of Saint Sergius (which inevitably fills with the waters of the flooding

Nile) served as the home of the Holy Family for seven years during their flight into Egypt. Nearby, a church dedicated to Saint Michael has replaced a synagogue, where it is said that Moses went regularly to pray, and the prophet Elijah appeared before the faithful from time to time in fleeting visions.

Like the Egyptian Jews, the Coptic Christians have withstood fourteen centuries of Muslim dominion, and have remained true to their metaphysical convictions; in diametrical opposition to the Jewish faith, however, they reject the human nature of Christ, and accept only his divine essence. The Coptic Museum is a repository of relics of centuries of stubborn faith; early Christian symbols appear on every object - sculptures and frescoes bear faded marks and bold emblems of such symbols as fish, grapes, and crosses. Icons, ceramic objects, and various accessories are on display alongside humbler objects, such as household wares and children's toys.

The Christians went from weakness to strength, and in A.D. 391 they burnt the Serapeum of Alexandria; in A.D. 537 they drove the priests from the temple of Isis on the island of Phylae - but neither the Christians nor any other religion has entirely succeeded in obliterating all traces of any other.

Time, which flows in an indolent and somewhat disorderly manner in this land, splits up and comes back together with improbable agility; in Egypt, three calendars are currently in use. The western calendar is used in scheduling business and official events; the Coptic calendar is based on the solar years since the time of the persecution ordered by the Roman emperor Diocletian (fourth century A.D.); the Muslim calendar, on the other hand, is based on lunar months, and dates from the year A.D. 622, the year of Mohammed's flight to Mecca, or Hegira. Perhaps a staid and predictable nation of musty Europe might have standardized the calendars and found some single compromise. But here time eddies slowly, talk is desultory and endless, and everyone stops for tea at five. The amiable Arabic code of manners deserves some compliance; at the worst, you will waste some time on flourishes and courtesy, and you may thus discover the secret mechanisms underlying the life of this "upside-down world." In the second volume of the "Histories," Herodotus notes a few oddities of the Egypt of his time: "The priests wear their hair long instead of shaven; women go to the market while the men stay home to weave, and they weave upward instead of downward; and one sits down to write, the letters progress from right to left instead of from left to right..."

Anyone who is willing to spend some time strolling through narrow alleys and streets in the Muslim neighbourhoods, in the Coptic quarter, or along the broad boulevards that have a hint of Paris, will have a series of remarkable impressions that jibe perfectly with the amazement of Herodotus. Men - or rather young men and boys - work at the weaving machines, and clothes are pressed by men, not women. Dance is often performed by men, and lithe male dancers, wearing long skirts, spin and sway to the furious handclaps of the clients (only men) of crowded cafes.

Religious observance fills the day, and there is a precise and closely obeyed schedule for prostration in prayer; at given moments throughout the day the entire nation, in offices, stores, and public streets, bows repeatedly in prayer to Mecca. If prayer is timely, nothing else is quite as punctual as in the anxiety-ridden west - a single phrase, mysterious and all-encompassing, serves to buffer all haste: "sabr gamil," or "patience is good." Westerners may mistakenly perceive as apathy what is actually indulgence and, in certain situations, a sublime stoicism. Gustave Flaubert certainly understood this when he remarked, to Abu Mandur while looking out over the Nile: "A boat under sail goes by, and there is the true East, with a sense of melancholy and drowsiness; one senses a great and implacable something from which there is no escape."

The stream of thoughts and observations about the Nile is as solemn and inexhaustible as the great river itself. "Egypt is a gift of the Nile," wrote Herodotus in 450 B.C., with reference to the periodic flooding that ensures fertility and wealth. "Nahal," or river valley, is the Semitic term which gives us the name of the river; the ancient Egyptians called the river "ar," from the word for black, to describe the silt which fends off the desert in a curving line. Some four thousand years ago, an Egyptian sang the river's praises in these words: "The Nile is father to life, a secret god risen from secret darkness, a god who floods fields, quenches the thirst of flocks, waters the earth, causes wheat to grow, and dispenses exquisite foods." The world's longest river flows for 4,160 miles, its course through the sand marked by a gaudy green line of fruit-laden palm trees, aromatic eucalyptus, and prized papyrus. The outlines of the hills overlap indistinctly, and the sun burns implacably over them in the blue sky. The dunes, instead, shift and drift, rising or settling as the Khamsin, or desert wind, changes direction and intensity. These "fifty-day winds" scorch the ground, dim the horizon, and rob farmland. The government does its best to fight back the choking arid waste, but the desert is vigilant and tireless. In the dry season, Muslims observe a month of fasting, Ramadan. Nature and the Koran agree - the root of the name of this month of privation and atonement is "ramz" - meaning "to burn." And Muslims can know no pleasures from dawn to dusk - though at nightfall the streets become lively again with the familiar colours. One event, in particular, contrasts with the ponderous flow of the ancient river - "sham e nesim," which translates, in a poetic admonition, as

26 top *Lake Nasser, formed by the Aswan Dam, flooded more than 190 square miles of northern Nubia, covering the sites of some of the world's most ancient archaeological finds.*

26 bottom *The construction of the Great Dam, officially named Sadd el-Ali, was planned between 1952 and 1954, with the aim of ensuring the water supplies and hydroelectric energy needed for the modern agricultural and industrial development of Egypt.*

27 top *Designed by the French engineer Ferdinand Marie de Lesseps, the Suez Canal was opened to shipping in 1869.*

27 bottom *The highway that leads from Aswan to Abu Simbel stretches through desert sands and crosses the Tropic of Cancer.*

28-29 *In this aerial view, the geometric plan of the Temple of Habo, near Luxor, harmonizes with the neat plots of farmland surrounding it.*

"Breathe the air of spring." Muslims and Copts gather together on the Monday following Easter (Coptic Easter follows Catholic Easter by one week) to observe this ritual as Nile-dwellers have for thousands of years: flower-laden boats pitch and roll on the dark waters of the Nile. The blue lotus, the white lotus, and a vast range of other flowering plants were mystical emblems of life in the cosmology of the pharaohs; modern Egyptians welcome the spring with food, not flowers. The feast in question is a mass picnic on the shores of the Nile. The Nile has, for many millennia, received the waters of Lake Victoria, the plentiful rains of the Ethiopian highlands, and with these waters, a vast harvest of exotic legends. Hapi (or Apis), the great lord of harvests, the god of fish, is incessantly present in the literature recorded on papyrus. He smiles at us, in an iconographic pose, with a pointed beard and a crafty expression, with women's breasts to symbolize fertility, and a handsome blue complexion. Popular belief considered Hapi to be responsible for the flooding of the river. According to mythology, Hapi possessed a bottomless pitcher, and from a cavern hidden in the mountains of Aswan, watchfully guarded by serpents, he would ceaselessly pour forth the bountiful water. Sacrificial animals were slaughtered by priests and farmers to win the god's good will and to keep him from distraction, for the slightest error in tipping the bottomless vase could result in massive flooding or disastrous drought. And the direction of the Nile's stream takes on some of the meaning of time's arrow; the imagination tends to move along it backwards, climbing ever southward - or "upriver," in the terminology of this upside-down land - while physical laws would have us moving northward, down toward the delta. Tour operators and cultural promoters of all sorts, of course, would steer us ever southward, toward Aswan and the monuments of the pharaohs; certainly, the average tourist is quite likely to miss entirely the delta region, and this is unfortunate. The fertile triangle that looks out over the Mediterranean is entirely devoid of charm in the traditional Egyptian sense. There are no towering sandstone monuments; they have been swallowed up by eons of silt or else destroyed to make room for croplands. The orderly countryside, endlessly green and dotted occasionally by infrequent palm groves, seems removed from the grip of the desert. Here, enterprising archaeologists search for the lost city of the Hyksos, solitary theologians retrace the steps of Biblical figures, and historians and philosophers delve into the earliest episodes of the hybrid Greco-Egyptian civilization that developed under the Ptolemaic dynasty. And sightseers from all over the world come to visit the second-largest city in Egypt, founded by an illustrious Macedonian warrior - Alexandria.

Universally considered to have been one of the

wonders of the ancient world, the city that bears the name of Alexander the Great possessed two harbours, a huge library, imperial palaces, great arsenals, and a huge lighthouse that guided the course of adventurous mariners from the peninsula where it once stood, now called Ras el-Tin. The ancient tradition of the Ptolemys makes Alexandria the cultural capital of the nation, while Roman culture enriched the city's identity with the prestige of conquering warriors (who were often conquered in their turn by Alexandria's charms). This fabled city, garish with merchandise and bartering, perched on the brink of the unknown, willingly offering its easy berth to passing sailors, suggests at the same time a meditative, introverted history of profound thought and poetic speculation, peopled by brilliant scholars hard at work in the chambers of the greatest library in history, now scattered to the four winds. The fifteen miles of beachfront are now crowded with giant umbrellas, bathers, and sun worshippers, mostly Cairenes, who seek to escape the crushing heat of summer with a dip in the refreshing waters of the southern Mediterranean. And the chaotic beachscape is mirrored by an equally jumbled cityscape. Contrasting with the deep blue of the sea is a jumbled line of fading and rundown vintage colonial buildings or modern architecture with bright colours. Among them, the majestic Abu el-Abbas mosque stands out, with its central octagonal structure which develops upward into towers and turrets, crowned with furbeloes and delicate parapets. The Nile flows out in two main branches, one at Damietta near Port Said, and the other at Rashid, once known as Rosetta, where in 1799 the shovel of an officer in Napoleon's expeditionary force clanked against the famed Rosetta Stone, the glossary that made it possible to decypher the impenetrable hieroglyphic alphabet. Let us leave Alexandria behind us - abandoning the site where the bite of an asp killed Cleopatra and yielded Egypt up to the power of the Egyptians, and where - in the battle of Aboukir - Lord Admiral Horatio Nelson finally broke the French fleet, and with it the absolute power of Napoleon. Let us go back up the river to Cairo, to the island of Gezira in the midst of the city, a fragment of land measuring two-and-a-half miles long by two hundred and fifty feet wide. Like in a set of Chinese boxes, in the heart of the city lies the key which allows us to unlock its meaning... Here stands a tower, built in 1961, which overlooks the capital of Egypt and the surrounding area which once was the city of Memphis. Here, the eye takes in what a zoning plan gone insane tends to scatter and jumble. The bird's-eye view, from atop a column encrusted with mosaics, reveals the personality - thoroughly schizophrenic, at first glance - of a city that succeeds in reconciling two contrasting, parallel cities; one is intricate, beetling, level with the river, and the other seems to be freeing itself

from the first, climbing up onto bridges, scaffoldings, and overpasses. Modern structures of cement and steel stand alongside other, equally monumental triangular structures made of sandstone and dust; to the north a jumbled skyline of bricks and rubble marks an ancient monument. Another heap of stones near the village of Mit-Rahineh is all that is left of the once magnificent temple of Ptah. These ruins, dating from the third millenium, formed the heart of the kingdom of the pharaoh Menes, who united the rival kingdoms of Upper and Lower Egypt into one. And the capital - then Memphis, now Cairo - grew and prevailed on a plain that lay at the boundary between the two former kingdoms. The stone of the rigid sculptures and the polychrome plasters and perishable papyrus documents all still bear the elegant symbols of the unification of the two kingdoms. Then as now, this was the nerve centre of Egypt; and the pharaohs who wore the crown of both kingdoms established their residence here, were buried here in great pomp and splendour, and built palaces and worshipped gods. The ancient Mennofer (Memphis is the Greek version) was the fortress against which invaders had to battle and the harbour which accumulated trade and wealth, the inevitable terminus for all merchandise and every request. From here, trains now set out for every destination for those who prefer to stay off the decks of boats or who want to retrace the steps of Pierre Loti, Agatha Christie, or T.E. Lawrence. In any case, a journey through Egypt is a journey along the Nile, preferably in a felucca, with its giant sails crossed like a shawl. The river served in ancient Egyptian religious beliefs as a highway connecting the world of the living and the world of the dead. Over the west bank, Amon-Ra, the deification of the sun, set while workers slaved in the necropolis to assure eternal life for their lost loved ones. And on the east bank, where the sun rose, they worshipped the renewal of life. Even today, the major hotels stand on the eastern bank, in an attempt to propitiate the gods of tourism. Visitors should see Thebes, Heliopolis - the "city of the sun," which boasted a thousand obelisks, the three great pyramids of Gizeh - upon seeing these massive structures, Napoleon calculated that they contained enough stone to surround all of France with a wall ten feet tall, Karnak where close to ninety thousand worked for the greater glory of Amon under the pharaoh Rameses III, and Abu Simbel, where the modern engineering of the High Aswan dam forced the eviction of the colossal statues of the pharaoh Rameses II...

Egyptian history is richer with every day that passes and, even for experts, is full of surprises and interest. The bowels of archaeological sites and cities of the dead will certainly not fail to yield up new questions on the enormous cultural heritage of the civilization of the Two Lands.

Buildings Made to Last for Eternity

Tons and tons of solid stone were cut, erected, and carefully set by skilled Egyptian builders as a challenge to the millennia. Massive slabs of rock were cunningly fitted together in some of the most daring architectural projects ever conceived by the human mind.
As we view these colossal constructions, we instinctively imagine modern techniques of planning and building, that are better suited to the enormous scale of these monuments.

But the architects drew up their plans using no tools more sophisticated than plumb lines, t-squares, yardsticks, and string; the huge armies of manual labourers moved the blocks of stone and heaved them into place using nothing more than earthen ramps, wooden sledges, rollers, and heavy tackle. All our hypotheses about construction methods remain hypothetical, and there are no documents to satisfy our curiosity; the Great Sphinx is the sole surviving witness, and continues to conceal the secret behind an enigmatic smile sixty feet from the desert sands.

30 top *The imposing complex of the temple of Karnak in Luxor dates back to the Middle Kingdom. In that time, it was the leading important shrine dedicated to the worship of the god Amon.*

30 bottom *Pierre Loti called the Island of Philae "the pearl of Egypt, one of the wonders of the world." He wrote a complete description of the island's monuments, later submerged and corroded by the waters of the artificial lake formed by the dam of Aswan. In 1980, these archaeological treasures were saved from further damage, and can now be visited on solid land, on the island of Agilkia.*

31 *On the plain of ancient Thebes, amidst cultivated fields, stand two tall, solemn statues, sentinels of an imaginary temple. They are the colossi of Memnon, seated on thrones, bearing the features of Pharaoh Amenhotep III, who had them built as guardians for his funerary temple, long since destroyed.*

The guardians of time

32 Earthen ramps, spiraling causeways, and other technical constructions were used in the completion of the audacious architectural projects of ancient Egyptian civilization. Scholars continue to guess at the exact methods used, without finding confirmation in any documents. The construction of the colossal pyramids of Gizeh is still a mystery of ancient engineering.

33 The Great Sphinx of Gizeh smiles enigmatically, overwhelming us with its limestone visage, over sixteen feet high, with an ear that measures four and a half feet in length. It stretches across the sand, 240 feet long. The Arabs who measured this colossus had little difficulty in thinking of a name: "Abu el Hol" - "father of terror."

34-35 In its original version, the Sphinx of Gizeh appeared on the horizon, red in colour, with a false beard on its chin and a sacred uraeus, or serpent, girding its forehead.

36-37 The Mastaba of Saqqarah, a funerary monument for King Zoser of the III dynasty, is built with six steps, each set back six and a half feet; it stands more than 180 feet tall.

Homage to Joy

According to Egyptian mythology, Hathor, goddess of love, dwelt in a sycamore tree. Thutmose III and Rameses II, pharaohs of the New Kingdom, began construction of a magnificent shrine, the temples of Dandarah, in which celebrations honouring Hathor could be held. Work on the temple continued under the Ptolemys, and under the Roman emperors Augustus, Domitian, Nerva, and Trajan. In 1799 a division of Napoleonic troops reached the temple while in hot pursuit of the Mamelukes, under the command of General Louis Charles Desaix; overwhelmed by the splendour of the temple, the general interrupted pursuit of his vanquished enemy in order to contemplate the building. The enterprising artist and archaeologist, Baron Dominique Vivant Denon copied down many of the inscriptions and reliefs; these were later studied by an expedition of fifteen scientists, in 1829, "captained" by Jean François Champollion. The founder of Egyptology wrote about the temple with great enthusiasm: "It represents the highest union between grace and majesty."

City with one hundred gates

In his *Iliad*, Homer hands down to posterity an image of Thebes as a rich and prosperous city: "A city with one hundred gates, each of them letting two hundred warriors with horses and carts pass through." The poet was rightly impressed by the imposing work carried out in the Temple of Luxor. Actually a great ambition pushed the pharaohs to carry out the project of this temple and the labour

required great care. Workers had different specializations: "hard labour" prisoners and prisoners of war were employed to mine for stone and the "easy" laying; stone-cutters showed their capability in carving the monoliths; expert surface cleaners prepared the bottom in order to get it ready for the last workers; draftsmen, engravers, and painters finished the work with their artistic contributions. Pillars, courtyards and arcades follow one another, developing the majestic temple in length. The huge papyrus-shaped columns are ever-present; in the peristyle seventy-four of them, placed in two ranks, can be counted.

Luxor, harem of the South

The Temple of Luxor is about 850 feet in length. It was built by Amenhotep III, a peaceful and enlightened pharaoh, during a period of great prosperity. The temple was enlarged by Rameses II, who had the first pylon and the first courtyard built. The first pylon is decorated with reliefs describing the battle of Qadesh, in what is now Syria, and in the first courtyard the seventy-four papyrus-shaped columns stand in rows, adorned with sixteen statues of the pharaoh. Along the northern side of the temple stands a chapel, dedicated to the worship of the three Theban gods: Amon, Mut, and their son, Khonsu. To the east, in the thirteenth century A.D., the mosque of Abu-el-Haggag was built. During the flooding of the Nile, the monumental complex came to life in celebration of the feast of Opet (known as the "beautiful feast of the harem"). A joyful procession trailed after the boat sacred to Amon from the temple of Karnak to "Amon's southern harem," as the temple of Luxor was called. In the time of Nekhtnebf I, during the XXX dynasty, the holy road that joined the two religious sites - known as the "dromos" - was crowded with hundreds of human-headed sphinxes, some of which still survive. During the New Kingdom, when many of the statues in the temple of Luxor were carved, sculptors began to strive after a more elaborate beauty. The beauty of the forms merged with the ideal qualities of stone - stability and durability - and were thus linked forever to the personality of the personage portrayed.

44-45 The pylon in the temple of Luxor was originally preceded by six colossal statues of Rameses II and by two obelisks made of pink granite. Now, only two statues of the pharaoh and one of the obelisks can be seen; the second obelisk stands in the Place de la Concorde, in Paris.

46-47 An impressive boulevard of ram-headed sphinxes leads to the first pylon, the main entrance to the temple of Luxor.

Pride of the Egyptian Pharaohs

These two emblematic views of the temple of Luxor seem to show clearly that sculpture had a deep religious meaning in ancient Egypt. The statues created for the temple either depicted a deity or else the faithful in prayer, and in both cases they bore "cartouches," or other indicators of identity. The artists of Memphis and Thebes, and in workshops in smaller towns, eventually developed refined technique, and learned to fulfil frequent and substantial orders. Quartzite, granite, diorite, porphyry, basalt, and sandstone were available in sufficient quantities to meet the inspiration of the craftsmen and the ambition of pharaohs. In 1903, a find in the temple of Karnak amazed both experts and laymen: during the excavations, G. Legrain found, next to the seventh pillar, a hiding place forty-six feet deep, which contained seventeen thousand bronze statues and 751 stone statues. The temple of Luxor stands, as the dedications say, "on ground adorned with silver, and lies on a foundation of incense," and beneath the stone slabs of the floor were hidden twenty-two statues of kings and deities, hidden by cautious priests. This hiding place under Amenhotep III's courtyard was chosen for both political and space-saving reasons. The statues found in this courtyard in 1969 are now kept in the museum of Luxor.

The faithful "servants of the square"

Deir el-Medina is a strip of land that squeezes in along the funerary temples west of Thebes and the along the mountainous area which conceals the Valley of the Kings. Deir el-Medina. It is a necropolis which afforded accommodation in the afterlife to those workers who belonged to an association, several millennia ago, called "servants in the Square." Quarrymen, sculptors, painters, carpenters, yard foremen, and manual workers buried at Deir el-Medina were the builders of the pharaohs' tombs, the tombs of the pharaohs' wives, and of their burial entourage. The tombs are crowned by small pyramids, the interiors are adorned with religious symbols that are universal to princes and commoners, as shown in these two photographs.

Creativity and tradition in six shades... the Egyptian art of color

52-53 The colour painting shown above is typical of the tombs of Rameses I and Horemheb, which can be visited in the Valley of the Kings. The Valley of the Kings is a huge necropolis built as a final and eternal resting place for the pharaohs of the XVIII, XIX, and XX dynasties. Palm fibre brushes, styluses with well-gnawed tips, water bowls and shells in which colours were mixed - this was the equipment of the craftsmen of Deir el-Medina who sure-handedly created nuances and refined effects, using the shades of charcoal black, chalk white, ochre red and yellow, and lively greens and blues obtained with sand and soda.

54-55 *Tourists entering the tomb of Tutankhamen are requested to show special respect and self-control, because the remains of both the child-king and of another pharaoh, Amenhotep I, were left in their original burial places. The bodies of both sovereigns were found by archaeologists in their tombs. Other pharaohs and notables however were less fortunate; their graves have been rifled and plundered repeatedly since ancient times. The looting began during the period of unrest that marked the end of the New Kingdom, and numerous royal mummies were moved by concerned priests to prevent vandalism.*

The boy-King

The heresy of the pharaoh Akhenaton (who was crowned as Amenhotep IV, but who changed his name to reflect the new monotheistic religion he introduced, centred around the god Aton) lasted only briefly, but revolutionized the Egyptian pantheon as well as arts and society. A young man was chosen by this Pharaoh as one of his daughters' husbands and his successor to the throne, and was given the name Tutankhaton. Upon the death of the older sovereign, the little prince's name, which meant, "Aton is of generous life," was changed to Tutankhamen, no doubt by the powerful priestly caste; the decree restoring the splendour of Amon (and abrogating the absolute power of Aton) was issued under his name. The young man, last pharaoh of the XVIII dynasty, died in the ninth year of his reign, at the age of eighteen. This youthful pharaoh, branded as a heretic and stricken from the official list of sovereigns for reasons of state, certainly seemed the least likely candidate for eternal fame. His tomb, however, in the Valley of the Kings, is the only one to have preserved its treasures intact until the twentieth century - every other tomb found to date has been plundered by thieves. In 1922, the archaeologist Howard Carter first entered the ancient tomb and wrote: "Time stood still here, and one wondered if the young king had been laid to rest with a joyful ceremony just the day before." Thirty-three centuries had, in fact, passed since that ceremony, but the furnishings, the statues, the gilded chapels, the pottery, the alabaster, the three sarcophagi, one within the other, and the garland of flowers crowning the boy's forehead had survived, intact and perfect.

56-57 The mask of Tutankhamen's mummy, shown in front and side views, bears the cobra and the vulture, deities of Upper and Lower Egypt; it also sports a false beard moulded in gold and covered with lapis lazuli, carnelian, and coloured glass.

A house built for giants

Karnak is the most solemn and majestic complex of temples to be found in all of Egypt. From the Middle Kingdom to Roman times, generation after generation of pharaohs worked to enlarge these temples, each striving to outdo his predecessors. An inscription tells us that the first temple built at Karnak dates from the first intermediate period (following the Old

Kingdom), but no trace of this first temple has yet been found. The most ancient monument dates back to the XIII dynasty; it is a cloister, and has been skilfully reconstructed by archaeologists. The most important buildings are enclosed by three huge walls made of sun-baked bricks; the giant Court of the Ethiopians gives onto the Arcade of Sheshonk, then Rameses's huge hall of hypostyles, and finally the obelisk of Queen Hatshepsut. Then there is the sanctuary of granite, the feast hall of Thutmose II, the temples of Khonsu, Opet, Mut, and Ptah. The architectural scale of the temples fits with the declaration of Jean-François Champollion: "The ancient Egyptians built as if they were 100 feet tall."

60-61 *Arrayed along an avenue, ram-like statues stand guard before the temples of Karnak. The ram was considered to be sacred to Amon, the patron god of Thebes.*

A royal tomb for a desert Queen

The funerary temple of Hatshepsut, with its balanced yet revolutionary structure, has no equal in Egypt. The terraced building, planned by the architect Senmut, rises majestically in the centre of a natural rock amphitheatre.

64-65 The necropolis of Thebes features the architectural magnificence of the temple of Hatshepsut - the powerful queen depicted with the manly appurtenances of royalty.

In Memory of Rameses, "Sun of Kings"

Northwest of the colossi of Memnon, one can visit the "Rameseum," a funerary temple built by Rameses to perpetuate his own memory and to glorify Amon. The outside wall has been destroyed and the great pylon knocked down, but the majestic ruins inspire the same respect as when they were new. A headless colossus of pink granite

portraying Rameses remains; it was originally fifty-nine feet tall and weighed over a thousand tons - nothing remains of it now but the torso and some rubble.

The pictures on this and the following page illustrate the imposing size of the temple of Ramses III; it is composed of two courtyards, each preceded by a pylon and a roofed section housing three hypostyle halls and a sanctuary. The first courtyard measures 112 by 105 feet, the second, 125 by 135 feet. The first pylon stands 207 feet long by 72 feet tall. A massive wall surrounds the entire complex, including the royal pavillion and the fortified entryway, with turrets topped by parapets. The temple boasts an unusual feature not found in monuments built at the same time; it has survived without the slightest modification. That a monument should remain faithful to the original architect's intent can be considered a singular piece of luck,

after the succession of generation after generation of pharaohs who, once they had conquered power, instantly - if figuratively - reached for their chisels, with the grim intent of cancelling the names and cartouches of previous sovereigns, substituting their own and thus winning credit for their construction. This architecture has a limitless value to scholars - on both interior and exterior, columns, walls, and porticoes bear scenes of great battles and religious worship. The statue above depicts the goddess Sekhmet, which translates as the "powerful one." She is portrayed with the features of a lion and was considered to be a particularly bloodthirsty divinity, responsible for epidemics and implacable in her destruction of the enemies of the sun.

Splendor and grandeur in the cult of Horus

On the left bank of the Nile, between Luxor and Aswan, the temple of Horus faces south; even from afar, one can clearly see its enormous length of four hundred and fifty feet. We know the date on which construction began from an inscription - 23 August, 273 B.C., during the reign of Ptolemy III. Imhotep, a priest and the architect of the temple, designed the building on the foundations of an older sanctuary. A number of pharaohs contributed to its construction until it was completed by Ptolemy XIII; this pharaoh is depicted on the pylon in the act of sacrificing prisoners to Horus. The temple is made up of a number of halls and chambers; like at Dandarah, one of these chambers was used as a workshop for the preparation of ointments and perfumes used in ceremonies. According to some cults, Horus - the hawk-headed god - was a deity of the air, in others a deity of the sky, and in others still, he is portrayed as the sun himself. Horus is shown wearing the double crown of Upper and Lower Egypt. In the temple of Edfu, consecrated to Horus, the wall decoration (seen on the following page) is quite remarkable - along the eastern wall of the long outer corridor which surrounds three sides of the temple, we see a visual narration of the legends concerning Horus and his birth, the way in which the god was to be worshipped, and the ceremony involved in laying the cornerstone of the temple.

The ancient Nubit
survives at Kom-Ombo

About thirty miles north of Aswan, on the right bank of the Nile, stood the city of Nubit. Now all that remains where the city once stood is the Graeco-Roman temple of Kom-Ombo, which is famous for its remarkable location, looking down over the river, and for the luminous brightness of the rock used in

building it. But it is something more than a romantic fascination that drives thousands of people to visit it each year: the temple is particularly intriguing because it was devoted to the worship of two gods - Sabek, the crocodile god, and Haroeris, the hawk-headed god. This dual nature resulted in double doors in the architecture and a very unusual appearance.

The Egyptians may have feared the crocodile with its terrifying tearing jaws, but their absolute vision of a harmonious universe did nothing to keep them from making it a god. In the fields of the delta and along the course of the Nile, Sabek, the crocodile god, had a great many worshippers, and numerous temples were built to him. Crocodilopolis, in what is now known as the Fayyum, was the capital of the spiritual realm of the crocodile cult, and a number of sacred crocodiles were kept there. Herodotus wrote this in his account of his trip to Egypt, and

confirmation is provided by Egyptian sources: "They keep these crocodiles as pets and they nourish them, they hang pendants of artificial stones and gold at the ears of these crocodiles, and bracelets on the forepaws; they feed them certain delicacies and victims, and they take the best care possible of them in order to let them live, and when they do die, they mummify them and bury them in sacred caskets."

Philae . . .
the pearl of Egypt

For over fifty years, the island of Philae, located near the first cataract on the Nile, showed its magnificent monuments for only a brief portion of each year. The rest of the time, the monuments were covered by the waters of the artificial lake formed by the old Aswan dam. The protests of Egyptologists went in vain, nor were

the heartfelt pleas of the romantic and men and women of letters to any avail. The problem was finally dealt with and solved when a further complication - the construction of the High Dam - added greater urgency to the matter. The waters between the two dams would have stayed at a constant level and, unless something was done immediately, the artistic heritage of the island might be lost forever. The work involved in dismantling the monuments lasted for two years. In November of 1976, the forty-five thousand blocks of stone taken from the island stood, out of danger, waiting patiently to be reassembled. The new location was to be the island of Agilkia, which had to be levelled and expanded so that the monument could be positioned correctly. The reconstruction was completed in 1979 by an Italian company.

On the island of Philae - which resisted as a stronghold of the old religion, stubbornly resisting the onslaught of Christianity - Nubian and Egyptian pilgrims brought offerings and sang hymns and intoned prayers to those deities long since rejected and forbidden (the last manifestation of the old religion was snuffed out in A.D. 473, and by that time all of the temples of Egypt had been converted to the new religion). The Isis cult fell before the blows of a different enemy, with an economic basis. For half a century, those who loved the temple saw it emerge from the waters, its cornices, the capitals of the pillars, and finally the generous soil arose to be covered with vegetation. For three months of each year, this spectacle rose from the water, and then the pylons, the colonnades, and the celebrated cloister of Trajan dropped back under the calm surface, like a Fata Morgana. Now, on the island of Agilkia, this structure can be seen all year, and tourists can rest in the cool shade of the portico of Ptolemy III. This temple, dedicated to Isis, took on great importance in antiquity since, not far off on the island of Biggeh, legend had it that the tomb of Osiris - the Abaton - stood, surrounded by three hundred and sixty-five offering tables, upon which a daily sacrifice of milk was left.

80-81 Ancient Egyptians made great use of wall carvings, and the ceilings, columns, and walls in the temples were completely decorated with figures carved in stone. The stone-cutters followed the rules of two-dimensional drawing but, by carving and shaping, they constructed scenes that will last forever. The wall carvings of the temple of Philae are shown here.

An enduring puzzle . . . the colossi

The temples of Abu Simbel are all that remain of the "colonial" city that stood here in Lower Nubia. In 1813, they were explored for the first time by the Swiss adventurer, Burckhardt. He succeeded in reaching the smaller one, before which stood six colossi, dedicated to the goddess Hathor, in tribute to the queen Nefertari, but he never managed to get to the larger one, which was dedicated to her husband, Rameses, because sand partially covered it and blocked the entrance. Later, the Italians Drovetti and then Balzoni tried to gain entrance, and the latter succeeded in 1917. Making his way into the giant monument, he gave the first description of the enormous hypostyle hall in which the complex narrative of the battle of Qadesh is set forth. The splendid building was finally completely freed of sand by Gaston Maspero.

82 *This photograph shows the temples of Nefertari and Rameses II, along with the nearby Lake Nasser.*

83 *Hundreds of workers laboured to extract from the limestone hillside the huge statues that the pharaohs set facing the sunset.*

Four huge colossi sit watching over the giant crater left in the limestone mountainside, once consecrated to the sun god Harakhte, Amon, and Rameses II. The cartouches of this sovereign appear on six rock temples in Nubia, and all over Memphis, Abydos, and Thebes. This immensely ambitious pharaoh may have reached the age of 100, and when he died, had founded numerous towns, fathered about a hundred sons, and led a sixteen-year-long war against the Hittites. His reign lasted sixty-seven years.

The masters of the East

Archaeologists and scholars tell us that the ancient Egyptians were so pleased with life on earth that their only complaint was that this life had to come to an end. The architecture seems fully in tune with this idea. If stone was quarried and transported great distances in order to give the dead eternal life, the living made use of a perishable building material - unbaked brick.

Along the fertile Nile Valley, and in the delta, innumerable cities once stood, now completely eradicated. The cities of Illahun, Tell-el-Amarna, and Deir el-Medina are some of the few that survive in the form of ruins. Tourist towns have sprung up alongside temples and archaeological sites such as Luxor and Aswan; others owe their existence to modernity. Port Said, Ismailia, and Suez have sprung up near the Suez Canal, and their economies fluctuate with the canal's business. Alexandria and Cairo have known both booms and busts, and the latter is now considered the cultural, spiritual, and political capital of the country and perhaps of the entire Arab world.

86 top *Merchants and sailors have figured greatly in the history of the Egyptian people; in Alexandria Fort Qaitbai is the site of a remarkable naval museum that documents the country's history. In this museum it is possible to see the oldest known ship's log, written on a scroll of papyrus.*

86 bottom *The El Khalil bazaar winds through the alleys of one of Cairo's oldest quarters. The dim shops are packed with all sorts of things made by local craftsmen, along with spices, scented oil, and textiles.*

87 *Cairo lies along the river Nile; this view shows the El Tahrir bridge and the Nile Hilton on the left.*

Marble mosques of scallops and "lace"

88 *Time spent in Cairo often involves little more than a tour of the ancient monuments, stripping the identity of Egypt of a fundamental and intriguing aspect: Islamic art. There are a great many mosques and madrasas - or religious schools each with a personality of its own. These buildings are designed with the shape of the tent of the nomad in the desert.*

89 Top left *The Ottoman mosque of Mohammed Ali was begun in 1824 and completed in 1857. The interior is lavishly decorated with alabaster, marbles, and polychrome inlay.*

89 Top right *The gracefully shaped cupolas of the numerous mosques, with their minarets, dominate the skyline of Cairo.*

Cairo . . .
the city of the sun

The pictures on these pages show how the Westernization of Cairo has come hand in hand with the population explosion. The tall buildings from colonial times, dignified and fading, are now joined by daring architecture with a rationalist look, to house the ever more numerous citizens of a rapidly expanding nation. The traffic grid is responding to the same imperative, with more and more lanes and unprecedented structural solutions. Apartments are shared, sublet; some thirteen million people are believed to live in the city, while another four million commute to jobs in Cairo each day, making use of public transportation and the city's space.

92-93 *A wide variety of goods fills the colorful Egyptian bazaar. Here it is possible to find precious jewels and large leather bags for water, and musicians and dancers add amusement to the eastern market.*

94-95 *The mystic Muslim doctrine* Suti *considers direct contact with God possible through ecstasy. In Al Hussein's camp, believers spend long periods of time on retreat.*

96-97 *At sunset, the "city with a thousand minarets" offers the camera an impressive view. In reality, the towers number only six hundred. Here the "priests" of the Islamic religion carry out their rites.*

The Hellenistic rise of
the second Egyptian city

Alexandria, the second largest city in Egypt, stands on a spit of earth, separated from the mainland by a large lagoon. It has two harbours - eastern and western. The former is the older, and now only small ships stop here; the latter is supplied with modern facilities that can accommodate large, heavy ships. All Egypt's imports come through Alexandria, a port with a history of thousands of years. It was founded by Alexander the Great in 332 B.C. Unfortunately, almost nothing remains of the city's Hellenistic past, because under Arab domination in the Middle Ages every trace of the Greeks was destroyed.

Luxor and Aswan . . .
secular attractions

100 *Luxor, with nearby Karnak the best known and most popular monument in Egypt, stands in the remains of ancient Thebes. Not far off is the immense necropolis, or burial ground, of the Valley of the Kings. One might envy the Egyptians this enormous and profitable tourist attraction; but one should bear in mind the enormous expense involved in the upkeep and preservation of these monuments.*

101 *The city of Aswan became a symbol of modern Egypt in the Sixties, with the construction of the spectacular new dam across the Nile. The Aswan Dam presented an unprecedented, two-fold challenge for both engineers and archaeologists. Just building the dam was a considerable engineering challenge, but saving the numerous and priceless monuments* *that would soon be engulfed by the rising waters of the Nile was an equally daunting task for archaeologists. Advanced technology was brought to bear in saving the temples of Da-Bod, Dendur, Kalabsa, El-Derr, Philae, and the two world-renowned temples of Abu Simbel from inundation. Experts and laborers from twenty-two countries, with financing from more than fifty* *nations, worked on this remarkable and successful project.*

Red Earth, Black Earth

Near the Nile's banks, the fertile black earth - called "keme" in centuries past - is the source of all life; just a few miles away lies the desert with its scorching red sands (once called "dosre"), the source of only silence and desolation.

The fertile land stretches only five to ten miles across, but extends over six hundred miles in length. The Nile delta covers an area of 115 miles by 155 miles. The animals and plants depicted and described in ancient Egyptian documents are long-forgotten legends to the modern inhabitants. Though the oasis of Al Fayyum, not far from Cairo, is still dotted with the marshes that were once exclusive royal hunting reserves, the crocodiles that once flourished there are now found only in Sudan; like that other denizen of the Nile, the papyrus, they are rapidly approaching extinction. An Egyptian of the Middle Kingdom would certainly be disconcerted by these changes; he would be reassured, however, by the familiar sight of the flocks of herons, egrets, and kite buzzards that darken the twilit skies over Gerizet, Nabatat (the Island of the Plants), or Abu Simbel.

102 top The course of the Nile near Aswan breaks into sharp turns and little islands, providing a little variety in the slow progress of the graceful feluccas.

103 bottom Both camels and oxen labour at ploughing the rich earth, driven by the Egyptian peasant, or "fellah."

103 The desert offers silence, desolation, and some unforgettable panoramas. By day, light and shadow interlock in an endless palette of colours; by night, the silent stars wheel overhead, sheltering the travellers who sleep in the sands.

Along the river . . .
the "flying swallows"

From the banks of the Nile, at Luxor and at Beni Hassan, the traveller can watch a slow procession of boats laden with freight and graceful feluccas, tossing and pitching with the swell, sailing under sails of all sizes. "The Nile is studded with broad white sails, set in crossed pairs that suggest a huge swallow in flight." That is how Gustave Flaubert described the Nile in his account of his journey to Egypt.

106-107 *The camera has captured, in a balanced and original composition, an exquisite slice of the river landscape.*

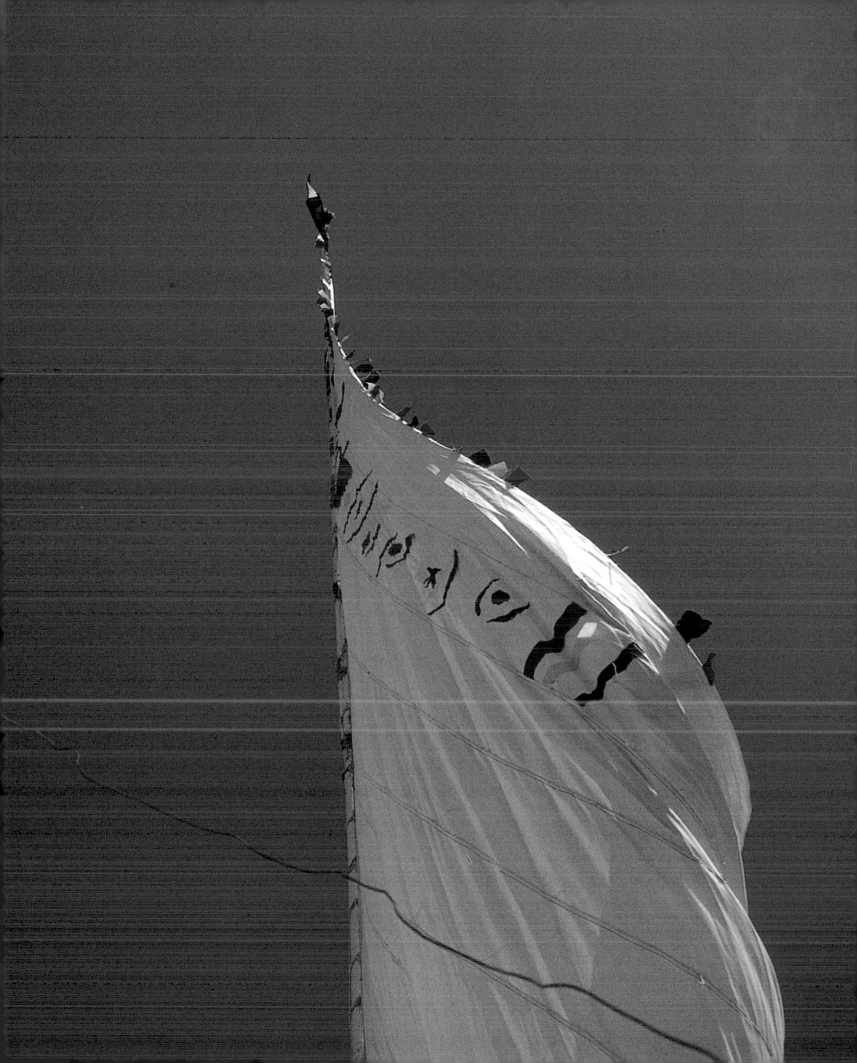

Green Are the Gifts of the River God, Hapi

The "Valley of Black Mud" has been farmed since the New Stone Age by peasants skilled at creating verdant landscapes. In past ages, the river yielded fertile crops or drought, at its whim. The "nilometers" (tall, clearly marked measuring sticks) that dot the valley landscape were closely watched; a perfect flood was announced when the water touched the height of sixteen cubits. The Egyptian government regulated irrigation and rationed the amount of water that each farmer could take for his plot of land. Now the Nile's floods are less a source of concern; the Aswan Dam assures a predictable flow of the waters that the ancient Greeks called the "rains of Zeus," and which the Egyptians attributed to the river god, Hapi. Little has changed, instead, in the tools used to irrigate the land and to harvest the crops. The water is still channeled through masonry wells, like those found near ancient temples; the water used to nourish the land is either taken from wells or drawn directly from the river by means of a "timbur," a traditional lever-operated machine that transports water with its unending circular motion.

110-111 *This bird's-eye view shows the remarkable landscape found in the small valley that stands at the southern tip of the necropolis of Thebes. The ancients described it, poetically, as the "Square of Beauty"; the Arabic language, thousands of years later, dubbed it "the gates of women." This burial ground is the feminine counterpart - far less magnificent - of the Valley of the Kings. Here the mortal remains of the daughters and wives of the pharaohs of the Ramesside dynasty were laid to rest. Within the valley, the geometric pattern of the neatly ploughed plots of land is broken here and there by isolated date palms.*

112-113 *Here we see an example of spontaneous, vernacular architecture in one of the many Muslim cemeteries at Abu Kerkas. In Egypt, Islamic culture obeyed the older tradition that relegated all the rites for the dead to the left bank, while the right bank was dedicated to a celebration of life.*

A Tradition
of Sharing

A Tradition of Sharing

114 This colourful house near Luxor must certainly belong to a "Hajj" - this word describes one of the faithful who has made the pilgrimage to Mecca.

115 The ritual of dining together brings a Bedouin family to a banquet of typical Arab dishes, made up

The Kingdom of Khamsin

The dunes of the Sahara desert shift in outline and contour, drifting ceaselessly with sharper or shallower slopes - an ongoing work of sculpture crafted by the desert winds. The caravan tracks that link a network of oases are often impassable, concealed beneath mountains of sand dumped by the powerful gusts. The desert is most

treacherous between March and June - the Khamsin, or "fifty days' wind," blows from the tropical lands to the south, from the tropical climates; the temperature rises sharply and whirling sandstorms blind the foolhardy traveller. In recent years, as the population has increased, demand for arable land has multiplied, and efforts have been redoubled to reclaim the desert. The Western Desert is now dotted with artesian wells, and the government offers the more daring farmers substantial financing so that they can work to make the arid desert fertile and green.

The gardens of the Red Sea

118-119 *The beach of Na'Ama (left) and the island of El Akhazein (known as the Island of Brothers, bottom) are treasure troves for those interested in marine plants and animals.*

These underwater photographs show a secret world, overlooked by those who take package tours, but familiar to expert divers. Portafaga, Hurghada, and Sharem el-Sheikh boast excellent diving facilities. Scuba divers and snorkellers can explore coral formations, iridescent tropical fish, and the myriad wonderful creatures that live in the waters of the Red Sea.

The land of the Bedouins

122 *The Arabs in these photographs are Sinai nomads, members of Bedouin tribes. The word Bedouin comes from the Arabic "Bedawi" - "desert dweller." Their appearance and customs seem unchanged over the millennia, living heirs to parables of the Apostles and Biblical traditions of exodus and pilgrimage, persecution and faith.*

123 *The expanse of dust and rock is broken only by sparse and hardy vegetation in the Sinai, near Sharm El Sheikh, the last tongue of land on the Red Sea.*

124 *The Greek Orthodox monastery of Saint Catherine in the Sinai desert was built in A.D. 527, on what was believed to be the site of the apparition of the Burning Bush before Moses, where God supposedly gave Moses the Tablets of the Ten Commandments. The emperor Justinian ordered the monastery built; the monastery boasts an illustrious past, and its library contains thousands of priceless manuscripts and a collection of ancient icons.*

125 top *The mountains of Sinai are, on average, 3,000 feet tall in the north and over 6,000 feet tall in the south; the tallest of them all is Mount Sinai, which stands 8,649 feet tall.*

125 bottom *From the monastery of Saint Catherine, it takes three hours to reach the peak of Mount Sinai, where a church has been built to commemorate God's gift of the Ten Commandments to Moses. Penitent monks have carved a 3,000-step stairway out of the solid rock.*

126-127 *Deep canyons and dizzying peaks distinguish the mountainous landscape of the Sinai, where Christian hermits took prayerful refuge.*

Photo credits:

Marcello Bertinetti / Archivio White Star: pages 118; 119; 121 bottom, 124; 125; 126-127.

DUBA: pages 26 bottom; 58; 86 top; 89 left; 92 top; 104-105; 108; 109; 112-113; 116 left; 120; 120-121 centre; 121 top; 122; 123; .

Ulrich Ackermann: pages 14-15; 88-89.

AGE Photo Stock: page 114.

Bond/Zefa: pages 114-115.

Christiana F. Carvalho/Apa Photo Agency: pages 116 right; 117.

C. Cerquetti/Panda Photo Agency: pages 60-61.

Arik Chan/Apa Photo Agency: page 92 bottom, top left.

Giuliano Colliva: pages 4-5; 6; 7; 10-11; 16; 17 bottom; 20 top; 20 bottom; 21 top; 22-23; 24-25; 30; 32; 33; 38;-39; 40; 41; 42; 43; 44-45; 46-47; 48; 56; 57; 59; 62-63; 64; 65; 66-67; 68; 69; 70-71; 72; 73; 74-75; 76; 77; 78-79; 80; 81; 82; 100; 101; 102.

Dallas & John Eaton/Apa Photo Agency: Cover; pages 1; 8-9; 17 top; 21 bottom; 27; 31; 50; 51; 52; 53; 54-55; 90.

Damm/Zefa: pages 18-19; 98-99.

First/Zefa: pages 2-3.

Cesare Gerolimetto: back cover, pages 28-29; 49; 103; 110-111.

Sylvain Grandadam/Apa Photo Agency: pages 34-35; 83; 89 right.

Robert Harding: pages 84-85; 96-97.

Richard T. Nowitz/Apa Photo Agency: pages 36-37; 106-107; 128.

Olive Sawyer/Zefa: pages 92-93.

K. Scholz/Zefa: page 87.

Sunak/Zefa: page 91.

Amedeo Vergani: pages 94-95.

Zefa Ialiana: pages 12-13.

Zefa/U.K.: pages 86 bottom; 91 top right.